ISLAMIC CREED

based on
Qur'ân and Sunna

ٱلعَقِيـدَة ٱلإسـلَامِيَّـة

مِنَ الكِـتَابِ وَٱلسُّـنَّـة ٱلصَّحِيحَة

By:

Muhammad bin Jamil Zino

Teacher in Dar-ul-Hadith Al-Khairiya
Makkah Al-Mukarramah

Maktaba Dar-us-Salam

Publishers and Distributors

Saudi Arabia • UK • USA • Pakistan

ALL RIGHTS RESERED

No part of this book may be reproduced or utilized in any form or by any means, electronic or mechanical, including photocopying and recording or by any information storage and retrieval system, without written permission of the publisher.

Copyright : All rights reserved
Printed in : 1995
Printing supervised by : Abdul Malik Mujahid
Printed at : Riyadh, Saudi Arabi

© **Maktabat Dar Usslam, 1995**

King Fahd National Library Cataloging-in-Publication Data

Zino , Mohammad bin Jamil
  Islamic creed based on Quran and sunna.
  .. p, .. cm
  ISBN: 9960-740-40-4
  I- Islamic theology   I- Title

240 dc   2378/15

Legal Deposit no: 2378/15
ISBN: 9960-740-40-4

Published by:

Maktaba Dar-us-Salam   . مَكْـــتَبة دَارالسَّـــلام
Publishers and Distributors   للنشـــــرِوالتَـــوزيع
P.O. Box 21441, Riyadh 11475   ص . ب . ٢١٤٤١ - الرياض ١١٤٧٥
Tel. 4033962 - Fax: 4021659   ت : ٤٠٣٣٩٦٢ فاكس : ٤٠٢١٦٥٩
Kingdom of Saudi Arabia   المملكة العربية السعودية

CONTENTS

PUBLISHER'S NOTE

Dear Readers,

Islam is the religion of truth revealed for the benefit of mankind for all times, all nations and all regions. Islam regulates the course of life to bring peace in this world and eternal success in the Hereafter.

In this book, all the important and fundamental aspects of Islam are described in an easy form of questions and answers so that the basic concept may be inscribed in the minds of the readers.

Dar-us-Salam feels great pleasure and honour in publishing the book according to its high traditions and standards. I am specially thankful to Mr. Shakil Ahmed As-Salafi, Hafiz Abdul Matin Rashid, Mr. Azmat Ullah, Mr. Ameen Arman and Dar Al-Khare of Jeddah for the special tasks of translation, title making, pasting, composing, proofreading and checking it with the original Arabic Book written by Mr. Muhammad bin Jamil Zino.

Abdul Malik Mujahid

General Manager

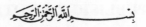

In the Name of Allah,
the Most Beneficent, the Most Merciful

All praise is due to Allah, we praise Him and seek His help, and beg His forgiveness. We seek refuge in Allah from the evil of our souls and from the wickedness of our deeds, whoever is guided by Allah cannot be led astray, and whoever is led astray shall find none other to guide him.

I bear witness that none has the right to be worshipped but Allah, Who has no partner, and I bear witness that Muhammad is His servant and Messenger.

These are some important questions about Islâmic Doctrine which I have answered, mentioning the proof-texts from the Qur'ân and correct and authenticated *Ahâdith* (true traditions and sayings of the Prophet صلى الله عليه وسلم) so that the reader may be satisfied with the correctness of the answers, since the Doctrine of Allah's *Tauhîd* (Monotheism, Oneness) is the foundation of man's happiness in this world and in the Hereafter.

I ask Allah to benefit the Muslims with this work and to make it purely for His sake.

Muhammad bin Jamil Zino

I. THE PILLARS OF ISLÂM

Q.1 **The Angel Gabriel asked: "Muhammad tell me about Islâm."**

A. The Prophet صلى الله عليه وسلم answered: Islâm is:

1. To bear witness that none has the right to be worshipped but Allah and that Muhammad is the Messenger of Allah (and that he was sent by Allah to teach us His religion).

2. And to establish *Salât* (prayer) — (that is to perform it correctly with sincerity and humility).

3. And to pay *Zakât*[1].

4. And to observe *Saum* (fasting) during the month of Ramadan — (by avoiding food, drink and sexual intercourse from dawn to dusk).

5. And to perform *Hajj* (to make pilgrimage to the House of Allah — the Sacred Mosque at Makka) if he/she is able to make this journey.

(Muslim)

---

[1] A certain fixed proportion of the wealth and of the each and every kind of the property liable to *Zakât* of a Muslim to be paid yearly for the benefit of the poor in the Muslim community. The payment of *Zakât* is obligatory as it is one of the five pillars of Islâm. *Zakât* is the major economic means for establishing social justice and leading the Muslim society to prosperity and security. [See *Sahîh Al-Bukhârî*, Vol. 2, Book of *Zakât* (24)].

II. THE PILLARS OF FAITH

Q.1 Gabriel asked: "Tell me about *Imân* (Faith)?"

A.   The Prophet صلى الله عليه وسلم answered: "Faith is to believe in:-

1. Allah
   [That He is the Creator and that only He has the right to be worshipped, and that He has Names and Attributes (referred to in the Qur'ân and *Sunna*) and that:

$$\text{﴿ لَيْسَ كَمِثْلِهِ شَيْءٌ وَهُوَ السَّمِيعُ الْبَصِيرُ ﴾}$$

   'There is nothing like unto Him, He is the All-Hearer, All-Seer'. (V.42:11)]

2. His Angels
   (Creatures of light, invisible to us, created by Allah, they perform certain duties assigned to them).

3. His Books
   (The Torah, the Gospel, the Psalms, and the Qur'ân which confirms and fulfills them).

4. His Messengers
   (The Prophets sent to mankind) The first was Noah and the last was Muhammad (peace be upon them all).

5. In the Final Day
(The Day of Resurrection when mankind will be judged).

6. And to believe in Allah's Decree (*Qadar*) both the good and the evil thereof.
(To be content with the fate which Allah has decreed for us, while taking the precautions and seeking the legal causes that lead to the desired purpose)."

(*Muslim*)

III. HUMAN BEINGS' DUTY TO ALLAH

Q.1 Why has Allah created us?

A. Allah has created us to worship Him Alone and to worship no other besides Him. The proof is Allah's saying:

﴿ وَمَا خَلَقْتُ ٱلْجِنَّ وَٱلْإِنسَ إِلَّا لِيَعْبُدُونِ ﴾

"And I (Allah) created not the jinns and humans except they should worship Me (Alone)." (V.51:56)

The Prophet صلى الله عليه وسلم said:

«حقُّ اللهِ عَلَى الْعِبَادِ أَن يَعْبُدُوه، وَلاَ يُشْرِكُوا بِهِ شَيْئاً» [مُتَّفَقٌ عَلَيْهِ]

"Mankind's duty to Allah is to worship Him Alone, and not to associate partners to Him in anything." (*Bukhâri - Muslim*)

Q.2 What is worship?

A. Worship is a comprehensive term which includes all sayings and actions which are appreciated by Allah; such as invocation, *Salât* (prayer), humbling oneself in front of Him etc. As Allah, the All-Mighty says:

﴿ قُلْ إِنَّ صَلَاتِي وَنُسُكِي وَمَحْيَايَ وَمَمَاتِي لِلَّهِ رَبِّ ٱلْعَٰلَمِينَ ﴾

"Say (O Muhammad صلى الله عليه وسلم): Verily, my *Salât* (prayer), my sacrifice, my living, and my dying are for Allah, the Lord of the *'Alamîn* (mankind, jinns and all that exists)." (V.6:162)

The Prophet صلى الله عليه وسلم said: "Allah says:

«وَمَا تَقَرَّبَ إِلَيَّ عَبْدِي بِشَيْءٍ أَحَبَّ إِلَيَّ مِمَّا افْتَرَضْتُهُ عَلَيْهِ» . [حَدِيثٌ قُدْسِيٌّ رَوَاهُ الْبُخَارِيُّ]

The most beloved things with which My slave comes nearer to me, is the observance of what I have enjoined upon him." (*Bukhâri*)

Q.3 How do we worship Allah?

A. We worship Him as He and His Messenger صلى الله عليه وسلم have commanded, as Allah says:

﴿ يَٰٓأَيُّهَا ٱلَّذِينَ ءَامَنُوٓاْ أَطِيعُواْ ٱللَّهَ وَأَطِيعُواْ ٱلرَّسُولَ وَلَا تُبْطِلُوٓاْ أَعْمَٰلَكُمۡ ﴾

"O you who believe! Obey Allah, and obey the Messenger (Muhammad صلى الله عليه وسلم) and render not vain your deeds." (V.47:33)

The Prophet صلى الله عليه وسلم said:

«مَنْ عَمِلَ عَمَلاً لَيْسَ عَلَيْهِ أَمْرُنَا فَهُوَ رَدٌّ» [رَوَاهُ مُسْلِمٌ]

"Whoever does any deed (in religion) which we have not commanded, it is rejected." (*Muslim*)

11

Q.4   Should we worship Allah with fear and hope?

A.   Yes, that is how we should worship Him as He has commanded His servants:

$$﴿ وَادْعُوهُ خَوْفًا وَطَمَعًا ﴾$$

"... And invoke Him with fear and hope ..." (V.7:56)

The Prophet صلى الله عليه وسلم said:

$$« أَسْأَلُ اللهَ الْجَنَّةَ، وَأَعُوذُ بِهِ مِنَ النَّارِ »   [رَوَاهُ أَبُودَاؤُدَ]$$

"I beseech Allah to grant me Paradise, and I seek refuge in Him from Hell-fire." (*Abû Dâwûd*)

Q.5   What is *Ihsân* (perfection in worship)?

A.   *Ihsân* (Perfection in worship) is to be conscious of Allah during worship. As Allah said:

$$﴿ الَّذِى يَرَاكَ حِينَ تَقُومُ ٠ وَتَقَلُّبَكَ فِى السَّاجِدِينَ ﴾$$

"Who sees you (O Muhammad صلى الله عليه وسلم) when you stand up (alone at night for *Tahajjud* prayer). And your movements among those who fall prostrate (along with you to Allah in the five compulsory congregational prayers)."(V.26:218,219)

The Prophet صلى الله عليه وسلم said:

$$« الإِحْسَانُ: أَنْ تَعْبُدَ اللهَ كَأَنَّكَ تَرَاهُ، فَإِنْ لَمْ تَكُنْ$$
$$تَرَاهُ فَإِنَّهُ يَرَاكَ »   [رَوَاهُ مُسْلِمٌ]$$

"*Ihsân* (Perfection in worship) is to worship Allah as if you are seeing Him, (and if you cannot concentrate to that extent) yet truly He is seeing you". (*Muslim*)

IV. FORMS AND BENEFITS OF *TAUHÎD*

Q.1 Why did Allah send the Prophets?

A. He sent them to call mankind to His worship and to reject the worship of anything besides Allah, as the All-Mighty says:

$$﴿ وَلَقَدْ بَعَثْنَا فِي كُلِّ أُمَّةٍ رَّسُولًا أَنِ اعْبُدُوا اللَّهَ وَاجْتَنِبُوا الطَّاغُوتَ ﴾$$

"And verily, We have sent among every *Ummah* (community, nation) a Messenger (proclaiming): ' Worship Allah (Alone), and avoid (or keep away from) *Tâghût* (all false deities etc. do not worship *Tâghût* besides Allah)'...." (V.16:36)

The Prophet صلى الله عليه وسلم said:

$$«وَالأَنْبِيَاءُ إِخْوَةٌ.. وَدِينُهُمْ وَاحِدٌ» [الْحَدِيثُ مُتَّفَقٌ عَلَيْهِ]$$

"The Prophets are brothers ... their faith is one." (*Bukhâri and Muslim*)

Q.2 What is the affirmation of Allah's Oneness as Lord? (*Tauhîd Ar-Rubûbiya*)

A. It is to affirm the uniqueness and exclusiveness of His works, creation and direction (of the universe) etc.

As Allah, the All-Mighty says:

$$﴿ الْحَمْدُ لِلَّهِ رَبِّ الْعَالَمِينَ ﴾$$

"All the praises and thanks be to Allah, the Lord of the *'Alamîn* (mankind, jinns and all that exists)." (V.1:1)

The Prophet صلى الله عليه وسلم said:

«أَنْتَ رَبُّ السَّمَوَاتِ وَالأَرْضِ . . »   [مُتَّفَقٌ عَلَيْهِ]

"You are the Lord of the Heavens and the Earth... " (*Bukhâri - Muslim*)

Q.3   What is the affirmation of Allah's Oneness as the Only One to be worshipped? (*Tauhîd Al-Ulûhiyah*).

A.   It is to devote to Him exclusively all our worship like; supplications, invocations, sacrifice, vows, prayer, hope, fear, seeking help, trust etc.

As Allah says:

﴿ وَإِلَٰهُكُمْ إِلَٰهٌ وَاحِدٌ لَّآ إِلَٰهَ إِلَّا هُوَ ٱلرَّحْمَٰنُ ٱلرَّحِيمُ ﴾

"And your *Ilâh* (God) is One *Ilâh* (God - Allah) *Lâ ilâha illa Huwa* (there is none who has the right to be worshipped but He), the Most Beneficent, the Most Merciful." (V.2:163)

The Prophet صلى الله عليه وسلم said:

«فَلْيَكُنْ أَوَّلَ مَا تَدْعُوهُمْ إِلَيْهِ، شَهَادَةَ أَنْ لَا إِلَـهَ إِلَّا الله» [مُتَّفَقٌ عَلَيْهِ]

"Let the first thing you invite them to do is to testify that none has the right to be worshipped but Allah."

14

وَفِي رِوَايَةِ الْبُخَارِيِّ: «إِلَىٰ أَنْ يُوَحِّدُوا اللهَ».

In another version in Bukhâri: "... to assert Allah's Oneness." (*Bukhâri - Muslim*)

Q.4 What is the affirmation of Allah's Names and Attributes? (*Tauhîd Al-Asmâ-was-Sifât*).

A. It is to affirm Allah's Attributes as He Himself describes them in the Book and as His Messenger صلى الله عليه وسلم describes Him in authentic *Ahâdith*, that they are true without allegorizing them (*Ta'wîl*), anthropomorphizing them (*Tajsîm*), comparing them to the creation (*Tamthîl*), or negating them (*Ta'tîl*) or questioning about their quality (*Takyîf*).

Such as the matter of (His) establishment (above the Throne), or (His) descent (to the first heaven) or (His) Hand, which are appropriate to Allah's Perfection.

Allah says:

$$﴿ لَيْسَ كَمِثْلِهِ شَيْءٌ وَهُوَ السَّمِيعُ الْبَصِيرُ ﴾$$

"There is nothing like unto Him and He is the All-Hearer, the All-Seer". (V.42:11)

The Prophet صلى الله عليه وسلم said:

$$« يَنْزِلُ اللهُ فِي كُلِّ لَيْلَةٍ إِلَى سَمَاءِ الدُّنْيَا »$$

[صَحِيحٌ رَوَاهُ أَحْمَدُ]

"Allah descends each night to the first heaven." (*Ahmad*)

15

(that is: He descends in a way befitting His Majesty, which is unlike the action of any of His creations).

Q.5 Where is Allah?

A. Allah is over the Throne (which is) above the (seventh) heaven. As Allah says:

$$ ﴿ ٱلرَّحْمَٰنُ عَلَى ٱلْعَرْشِ ٱسْتَوَىٰ ﴾ $$

"The Most Beneficent (Allah) *Istawa* (rose over) the (Mighty) Throne (in a manner that suits His Majesty)." (V.20:5)

(that is: He raised Himself above it).

The Prophet صلى الله عليه وسلم said:

$$ إِنَّ اللهَ كَتَبَ كِتَابًا قَبْلَ أَنْ يَخْلُقَ الْخَلْقَ . . . فَهُوَ مَكْتُوْبٌ عِنْدَهُ فَوْقَ الْعَرْشِ ﴾ [رَوَاهُ الْبُخَارِيُّ] $$

"Allah wrote out (all things) in a Book before He created the creation .... it is with Him above the Throne." (*Bukhâri*)

Q.6 Is Allah with us?

A. Allah is with us through His Knowledge (of all things). He hears and sees us, as He says:

$$ ﴿ قَالَ لَا تَخَافَا إِنَّنِي مَعَكُمَا أَسْمَعُ وَأَرَىٰ ﴾ $$

"He (Allah) said: Fear not, Verily! I am with you both, Hearing and Seeing." (V.20:46)

The Prophet صلى الله عليه وسلم said:

«إِنَّكُمْ تَدْعُونَ سَمِيعًا قَرِيبًا وَهُوَ مَعَكُمْ» (أَيْ بِعِلْمِهِ)
[رَوَاهُ مُسْلِمٌ]

"... You call upon the One Who hears, Who is near, and is with you (i.e. through His Knowledge)." (*Muslim*)

Q.7 What is the benefit of affirming Allah's Oneness (*Tauhîd*)?

A. It is salvation from eternal punishment in the Hereafter, right guidance in this world, and forgiveness for sin. Allah, the All-Mighty says:

﴿ٱلَّذِينَ ءَامَنُوا۟ وَلَمْ يَلْبِسُوٓا۟ إِيمَٰنَهُم بِظُلْمٍ أُو۟لَٰٓئِكَ لَهُمُ ٱلْأَمْنُ وَهُم مُّهْتَدُونَ﴾

"It is those who believe (in the Oneness of Allah and worship none but Him Alone) and confuse not their belief with *Zulm* (wrong i.e. by worshipping others besides Allah), for them (only) there is security and they are guided." (V.6:82)

The Prophet صلى الله عليه وسلم said:

«حَقُّ الْعِبَادِ عَلَى اللهِ أَنْ لاَ يُعَذِّبَ مَنْ لاَّ يُشْرِكُ بِهِ شَيْئًا» [مُتَّفَقٌ عَلَيْهِ]

"The worshipper's right on Allah is that He will not punish those who worship none besides Him." (*Bukhâri* and *Muslim*)

17

V. CONDITIONS FOR ALLAH'S ACCEPTANCE OF OUR DEEDS

Q.1 **What are the conditions for the acceptance of our deeds?**

A. They are three:

1. Belief (Faith) in Allah and affirmation of His Oneness, as Allah says:

$$﴿ إِنَّ ٱلَّذِينَ ءَامَنُوا۟ وَعَمِلُوا۟ ٱلصَّٰلِحَٰتِ كَانَتْ لَهُمْ جَنَّٰتُ ٱلْفِرْدَوْسِ نُزُلًا ﴾$$

"Verily! Those who believe (in the Oneness of Allah — Islâmic Monotheism) and do righteous deeds, shall have the Gardens of *Al-Firdaus* (Paradise) for their entertainment". (V.18:107)

The Prophet ﷺ said:

$$«قُلْ آمَنْتُ بِاللهِ ثُمَّ اسْتَقِمْ» [رَوَاهُ مُسْلِمٌ]$$

2. Sincerity (*Ikhlâs*), which is to do deeds for Allah's sake only neither seeking praise from fellow-beings nor to have repute among men. Allah says:

$$﴿ فَٱدْعُوا۟ ٱللَّهَ مُخْلِصِينَ لَهُ ٱلدِّينَ ﴾$$

"So, call you (O Muhammad ﷺ and the believers) upon (or invoke) Allah making (your) worship pure for Him (Alone) (by worshipping none but Him and by doing religious deeds sincerely for Allah's sake only and not to show off and not to set up rivals with Him in

18

worship)." (V.40:14)

The Prophet صلى الله عليه وسلم said:

«مَنْ قَالَ لا إِلَـهَ إِلا اللهُ مُخْلِصاً دَخَلَ الْجَنَّةَ»

[صَحِيحٌ رَوَاهُ الْبَزَّارُ وَغَيْرُهُ]

"Whoever sincerely testifies: 'None has the right to be worshipped but Allah' shall enter Paradise." (*Al-Bazzâr* and others)

3. That they should be in accordance with the teachings of Allah's Messenger صلى الله عليه وسلم , as Allah says:

﴿ وَمَآ ءَاتَىٰكُمُ ٱلرَّسُولُ فَخُذُوهُ وَمَا نَهَىٰكُمْ عَنْهُ فَٱنتَهُوا ﴾

"... And whatsoever the Messenger (Muhammad صلى الله عليه وسلم) gives you, take it, and whatsoever he forbids you, abstain (from it) ... " (V.59:7)

The Prophet صلى الله عليه وسلم said:

«مَنْ عَمِلَ عَمَلاً لَيْسَ عَلَيْهِ أَمْرُنَا فَهُوَ رَدٌّ»

(أَىْ غَيْرُ مَقْبُولٍ) [رَوَاهُ مُسْلِمٌ]

"Whoever does any deed (in religion) which we have not commanded, it is rejected." (*Muslim*)

19

VI. MAJOR *SHIRK (SHIRK AKBAR)*[1] AND ITS MANIFESTATIONS

Q.1 What is major *Shirk*?

A. It is to devote any of the forms of worship to one other than Allah, such as supplication, invocation, sacrifice, etc. The proof-text is Allah's Saying:

﴿ وَلَا تَدْعُ مِن دُونِ ٱللَّهِ مَا لَا يَنفَعُكَ وَلَا يَضُرُّكَ فَإِن فَعَلْتَ فَإِنَّكَ إِذًا مِّنَ ٱلظَّـٰلِمِينَ ﴾

"And invoke not besides Allah, any that neither profit you, nor hurt you, but if (in case) you did so, you shall certainly be one of the *Zâlimûn* (polytheists and wrong-doers)." (V.10:106)

The Prophet صلى الله عليه وسلم said:

«أَكْبَرُ الْكَبَائِرِ: الإِشْرَاكُ بِاللهِ وَعُقُوقُ الْوَالِدَيْنِ، وَشَهَادَةُ الزُّورِ» [رَوَاهُ مُسْلِمٌ]

"The greatest sins are joining others with Allah in worship, disobedience to parents and to give false evidence." (*Muslim*)

Q.2 What is the greatest sin with Allah?

A. The greatest sin with Allah is to commit major *Shirk*, the proof-text is Allah's Saying: recalling the

---

[1] *Shirk* implies ascribing partners to Allah or ascribing divine attributes to others besides Allah and believing that the source of power, harm, and blessings comes from another besides Allah.

20

words of Luqman to his son:

$$ ﴿ يَـٰبُنَىَّ لَا تُشْرِكْ بِٱللَّهِ إِنَّ ٱلشِّرْكَ لَظُلْمٌ عَظِيمٌ ﴾ $$

"O my son! Join not in worship others with Allah. Verily! Joining others in worship with Allah is great *Zulm* (wrong) indeed." (V. 31:13)

When Allah's Messenger was asked which is the greatest sin, he answered:

$$ «أَنْ تَجْعَلَ لِلهِ نِدًّا وَهُوَ خَلَقَكَ» [مُتَّفَقٌ عَلَيْهِ] $$

"To ascribe partners with Allah even though He Alone created you." (*Bukhâri* and *Muslim*)

Q.3 Does *Shirk* exist among Muslims today?

A.   Yes, it does exist, the proof-text being Allah's Saying:

$$ ﴿ وَمَا يُؤْمِنُ أَكْثَرُهُم بِٱللَّهِ إِلَّا وَهُم مُّشْرِكُونَ ﴾ $$

"And most of them believe not in Allah, except that they attribute partners (unto Him i.e. they are *Mushrikun* - polytheists)." (V.12:106)

The Prophet صلى الله عليه وسلم said:

$$ «لَا تَقُومُ السَّاعَةُ حَتَّى تَلْحَقَ قَبَائِلُ مِنْ أُمَّتِي بِالْمُشْرِكِينَ وَحَتَّى تُعْبَدَ الأَوْثَانُ» [صَحِيحٌ رَوَاهُ التِّرْمِذِيُّ] $$

"The Doomsday will not occur until some sections of my people have joined the idolaters and they will even worship idols." (*Tirmidhi*)

Q.4 **What is the ruling concering praying (supplicating) to the dead or those who are absent?**

A. Praying to them is a major *Shirk*, as Allah says:

$$﴿ فَلَا تَدْعُ مَعَ ٱللَّهِ إِلَٰهًا ءَاخَرَ فَتَكُونَ مِنَ ٱلْمُعَذَّبِينَ ﴾$$

"Invoke not with Allah another *Ilâh* (god) lest you be among those who receive punishment." (V.26:213)

The Prophet ﷺ said:

«مَنْ مَاتَ وَهُوَ يَدْعُو مِنْ دُوْنِ الله نِدًّا دَخَلَ النَّارَ»

[رَوَاهُ الْبُخَارِيُّ]

"Whoever dies having called upon partners besides Allah shall enter Hell-fire." (*Bukhâri*)

Q.5 **Is supplication a form of worship?**

A. Yes, supplication is worship, as Allah says:

$$﴿ وَقَالَ رَبُّكُمُ ٱدْعُونِىٓ أَسْتَجِبْ لَكُمْ إِنَّ ٱلَّذِينَ يَسْتَكْبِرُونَ عَنْ عِبَادَتِى سَيَدْخُلُونَ جَهَنَّمَ دَاخِرِينَ ﴾$$

"And your Lord said: Invoke Me, [i.e. believe in My Oneness (Islâmic Monotheism)] (and ask Me for anything) I will respond to your (invocation). Verily! Those who scorn My worship [i.e. do not invoke Me, and do not believe in My Oneness, (Islâmic Monotheism)] they will surely enter Hell in humiliation!" (V. 40: 60)

The Prophet صلى الله عليه وسلم said:

$$\text{«اَلدُّعَاءُ هُوَ الْعِبَادَةُ» [رَوَاهُ التِّرْمِذِي وَقَالَ حَسَنٌ صَحِيْحٌ]}$$

"Supplication is worship." (*Tirmidhi*)

Q.6 Do the dead hear our supplications?

A.   No, they do not hear, as Allah said:

$$\text{﴿ وَمَا أَنتَ بِمُسْمِعٍ مَّن فِي ٱلْقُبُورِ ﴾}$$

"... But you cannot make hear those who are in graves." (V.35:22)

Ibn 'Umar رضي الله عنهما says: The Prophet صلى الله عليه وسلم stood at the graves of the idolaters at Badr and recited:

$$\text{﴿ فَهَلْ وَجَدتُّم مَّا وَعَدَ رَبُّكُمْ حَقًّا ﴾}$$

"... Have you also found true, what your Lord promised (warnings, etc.) ... " (V.7:44)

Then he said:

$$\text{«إِنَّهُمُ الآنَ يَسْمَعُوْنَ مَا أَقُوْلُ»}$$

"They now hear what I say".

When this was mentioned to 'Aisha رضي الله عنها , she said: The Prophet صلى الله عليه وسلم only said that:

$$\text{«إِنَّهُمُ الآنَ لَيَعْلَمُوْنَ، أَنَّمَا كُنْتُ أَقُوْلُ لَهُمْ هُوَ الْحَقُّ»}$$

"now they shall know that what I used to tell them was the truth."

23

She then recited (this verse):

$$﴿ إِنَّكَ لَا تُسْمِعُ ٱلْمَوْتَىٰ ﴾$$

"You cannot make the dead to hear ..." (V.27:80)

وقال قتادة راوي الحديث : « أَحْيَاهُمُ اللهُ حَتَّى

أَسْمَعَهُمْ قَوْلَهُ تَوْبِيخاً وَتَصْغِيرًا، وَنَقِيمَةً وَحَسْرَةً

وَنَدَامَةً » [رواه البخاري]

Qatadah, the narrator of this *Hadith* (from Ibn 'Umar) said: "Allah brought them to life to make them hear the words of the Prophet as a rebuke and humiliation." (*Bukhari*)

This *Hadîth* teaches:

1. That these idolaters slain (at Badr) were caused to hear temporarily by the Order of Allah. This is proven by the Prophet's saying:

    «إِنَّهُمُ الآنَ يَسْمَعُوْنَ»

    "Now they can hear" , which implies that later they will no longer hear, as Qatadah, the narrator of the *Hadith* said: "Allah brought them to life to make them hear His Words as a rebuke and humiliation..."

2. 'Aisha's refutation of Ibn 'Umar's version that the Prophet صلى الله عليه وسلم did not say:

    «يَسْمَعُوْنَ»   بل قال «إِنَّهُمُ الآنَ يَعْلَمُوْنَ»

    "They can hear" but rather that he said: "Now they

know" was based on the verse:

$$\text{﴿ إِنَّكَ لَا تُسْمِعُ ٱلْمَوْتَىٰ ﴾}$$

"Verily, you cannot make the dead to hear ..." (V.27:80)

3. The versions of Ibn 'Umar and 'Aisha can be harmonized in the following manner:

The fact is, that the dead cannot hear; as is plainly stated by the Qur'ân, but Allah brought to life the idolaters slain (at Badr) miraculously for the Messenger's sake, so that they could hear him — as Qatadah, the narrator of the *Hadîth* states — and Allah knows best.

VII. TYPES OF MAJOR *SHIRK* (*SHIRK AKBAR*)

Q.7 Should we seek help from those who are dead, or from those who are not present?

A. No, we should not seek their help, rather we should seek the help of Allah, as He says:

﴿ وَٱلَّذِينَ يَدْعُونَ مِن دُونِ ٱللَّهِ لَا يَخْلُقُونَ شَيْئًا وَهُمْ يُخْلَقُونَ ۝ أَمْوَٰتٌ غَيْرُ أَحْيَآءٍ وَمَا يَشْعُرُونَ أَيَّانَ يُبْعَثُونَ ﴾

"Those whom they (*Al-Mushrikûn*) invoke besides Allah have not created anything, but are themselves created. (They are) dead, lifeless, and they know not when they will be raised up." (V.16:20,21)

﴿ إِذْ تَسْتَغِيثُونَ رَبَّكُمْ فَٱسْتَجَابَ لَكُمْ ﴾

"(Remember) when you sought help of your Lord and He answered you." (V.8:9)

The Prophet صلى الله عليه وسلم prayed:

«يَا حَيُّ يَا قَيُّومُ، بِرَحْمَتِكَ أَسْتَغِيثُ»

[حَسَنٌ رَوَاهُ التِّرْمِذِيُّ]

"O the Everliving, the Everlasting Allah, I seek help through Your Mercy". (*Tirmidhi*)

Q.8 Is it permitted to seek help from any other besides Allah?

A. No, it is not permitted, the evidence is Allah's

Saying:

$$\lllangle \text{إِيَّاكَ نَعْبُدُ وَإِيَّاكَ نَسْتَعِينُ} \rrrangle$$

"You (Alone) we worship, and You (Alone) we ask for help (for each and everything)." (V.1:5)

The Prophet صلى الله عليه وسلم said:

«إِذَا سَأَلْتَ فَاسْأَلِ اللهَ، وَإِذَا اسْتَعَنْتَ فَاسْتَعِنْ بِاللهِ»
[رَوَاهُ التِّرْمِذِيُّ وَقَالَ حَسَنٌ صَحِيحٌ]

"If you ask, ask of Allah, if you seek help, seek help of Allah". (*Tirmidhi*)

Q.9 May we seek help from the living?

A. Yes, in the matters in which they are able (to help), as Allah says:

$$\lllangle \text{وَتَعَاوَنُوا عَلَى الْبِرِّ وَالتَّقْوَى} \rrrangle$$

"... Help you one another in *Al-Birr* and *At-Taqwa* (virtue, righteousness and piety) ... " (V.5:2)

The Prophet صلى الله عليه وسلم said:

«وَاللهُ فِي عَوْنِ الْعَبْدِ، مَا كَانَ الْعَبْدُ فِي عَوْنِ أَخِيهِ» [رَوَاهُ مُسْلِمٌ]

"Allah helps His worshipper as long as the worshipper helps his brother." (*Muslim*)

27

Q.10 Is it permitted to swear oaths (make vows) to any other besides in the Name of Allah?

A. No, it is not permitted to swear oaths except in Allah's Name, as Allah mentions the words of Mary's mother:

$$ ﴿ رَبِّ إِنِّي نَذَرْتُ لَكَ مَا فِي بَطْنِي مُحَرَّرًا ﴾ $$

"... O my Lord! I have vowed to You what (the child that) is in my womb to be dedicated for Your services (free from all worldly work; to serve Your Place of worship), ..." (V.3:35)

The Prophet صلى الله عليه وسلم said:

$$ « مَنْ نَـذَرَ أَنْ يُطِيـعَ اللهَ فَلْيُطِعْـهُ، وَمَنْ نَـذَرَ أَنْ $$
$$ يَعْصِيَهُ، فَلَا يَعْصِهِ » [رَوَاهُ الْبُخَارِيُّ] $$

"Whoever vows to obey Allah should obey Him, and whoever vows to disobey Him should not disobey." (*Bukhâri*)

Q.11 Is it permitted to sacrifice in any name besides Allah?

A. No, it is not permitted, the proof is Allah's Saying:

$$ ﴿ فَصَلِّ لِرَبِّكَ وَانْحَرْ ﴾ $$

"Therefore turn in prayer to your Lord and sacrifice (to Him only)." (V.108:2)

(To sacrifice is to slaughter an animal for food in Allah's Name).

The Prophet صلى الله عليه وسلم said:

«لَعَنَ اللهُ مَنْ ذَبَحَ لِغَيْرِ اللهِ» [رَوَاهُ مُسْلِمٌ]

"Allah curses whoever sacrifices and slaughters in any name other than Allah." (*Muslim*)

Q.12 Is it permitted to circumambulate any other structure besides the Ka'ba?

A. No, it is not permitted to circumambulate any other structure besides the Ka'ba, as Allah says:

﴿ وَلْيَطَّوَّفُواْ بِٱلْبَيْتِ ٱلْعَتِيقِ ﴾

"... And circumabulate the Ancient House (the Ka'ba at Makka)." (V.22:29)

The Prophet صلى الله عليه وسلم said:

«مَنْ طَافَ بِالْبَيْتِ سَبْعًا وَصَلَّى رَكْعَتَيْنِ، كَانَ كَعِتْقِ رَقَبَةٍ» [صَحِيحٌ رَوَاهُ ابْنُ مَاجَه]

"Whoever circumambulate the House (the Ka'ba) seven times and prays two *Rak'a* of *Salât*, it is as if he has freed a slave." (*Ibn Mâjah*)

Q.13 What is the ruling in Islâm concerning (the practice of) magic/sorcery?

A. The practice of magic/sorcery is considered rejection of faith (*Kufr*), as Allah said:

﴿ وَلَـٰكِنَّ ٱلشَّيَـٰطِينَ كَفَرُواْ يُعَلِّمُونَ ٱلنَّاسَ ٱلسِّحْرَ ﴾

"... But the devils disbelieved, teaching men magic..." (V. 2:102)

The Prophet صلى الله عليه وسلم said:

$$\text{« اجْتَنِبُوا السَّبْعَ الْمُوبِقَاتِ: الشِّرْكُ بِاللهِ،}$$

$$\text{وَالسِّحْرُ ... »} \quad [\text{الْحَدِيثَ رَوَاهُ مُسْلِمٌ}]$$

"Avoid seven deadly sins; *Shirk*, magic ... "
(*Muslim*)

Q.14 Should we believe the claims of fortunetellers and soothsayers (*Kâhin*)?

A.   No, we should not believe them, as Allah says:

$$\text{﴿ قُل لَّا يَعْلَمُ مَن فِي السَّمَوَاتِ وَالْأَرْضِ الْغَيْبَ إِلَّا اللَّهُ ﴾}$$

"Say: "None in the heavens and the earth knows the *Ghaib* (unseen) except Allah, ... " (V.27:65)

The Prophet صلى الله عليه وسلم said:

$$\text{«مَنْ أَتَى عَرَّافاً، أَوْ كَاهِنًا، فَصَدَّقَهُ بِمَا يَقُولُ، فَقَدْ كَفَرَ بِمَا}$$

$$\text{أُنْزِلَ عَلَى مُحَمَّدٍ»} \quad [\text{صَحِيحٌ رَوَاهُ أَحْمَدُ}]$$

"Whoever goes to a fortuneteller or a soothsayer, and believes what they say, has rejected what has been revealed to Muhammad." (*Ahmad*)

Q.15 Does anyone have knowledge of the unseen?

A.   No, no one but Allah Alone has knowledge of the unseen. Allah says (referring to Himself):

$$\text{﴿ وَعِندَهُ مَفَاتِحُ الْغَيْبِ لَا يَعْلَمُهَا إِلَّا هُوَ ﴾ ...}$$

"And with Him are the keys of the *Ghaib* (all that is hidden), none knows them but He. And He knows

30

whatever there is in (or on) the earth and in the sea; not a leaf falls, but he knows it. There is not a grain in the darkness of the earth nor anything fresh or dry, but is written in a Clear Record." (V.6:59)

The Prophet صلى الله عليه وسلم said:

«لاَ يَعْلَمُ الْغَيْبَ إلا اللهُ» [حَسَنٌ رَوَاهُ الطَّبَرَانِيُّ]

"No one has knowledge of the unseen except Allah." (*Tabarâni*)

Q.16 What is the ruling in Islâm concerning applying non-Islâmic laws?

A. Abiding the laws which are contrary to Islâm and accepting them as superior to Islâmic Laws is rejection of Faith. Allah says:

﴿ وَمَن لَّمْ يَحْكُم بِمَآ أَنزَلَ ٱللَّهُ فَأُوْلَٰٓئِكَ هُمُ ٱلْكَٰفِرُونَ ﴾

"... And whosoever does not judge by what Allah has revealed, such are the *Kâfirûn* (i.e. disbelievers — of a lesser degree as they do not act on Allah's Laws)." (V.5:44)

The Prophet صلى الله عليه وسلم said:

«وَمَا لَمْ تَحْكُمْ أَئِمَّتُهُمْ بِكِتَابِ اللهِ، وَيَتَخَيَّرُوا مِمَّا أَنْزَلَ اللهُ، إلَّا جَعَلَ اللهُ بَأْسَهُمْ بَيْنَهُمْ»

[حَسَنٌ رَوَاهُ ابْنُ مَاجَه وَغَيْرُهُ]

"When the leaders do not rule by Allah's Book (Qur'ân) and choose from that which Allah has

31

rejected, Allah will cause conflict among them."
(*Ibn Mâjah*)

Q.17 What if Satan tempts us with the question: "Who created Allah"?

A. If Satan tempts you with this question you should seek refuge in Allah, as Allah says:

$$ ﴿ وَإِمَّا يَنزَغَنَّكَ مِنَ ٱلشَّيْطَانِ نَزْغٌ فَٱسْتَعِذْ بِٱللَّهِ إِنَّهُ هُوَ ٱلسَّمِيعُ ٱلْعَلِيمُ ﴾ $$

"And if an evil whisper from Satan tries to turn you away (O Muhammad صلى الله عليه وسلم) (from doing good etc.), then seek refuge in Allah. Verily, He is the All-Hearer, the All-Knower." (V.41:36)

Allah's Messenger صلى الله عليه وسلم taught us to resist Satan's deceptions by saying:

«آمَنْتُ بِاللهِ وَرُسُلِهِ، اللهُ أَحَدٌ، اللهُ الصَّمَدُ، لَمْ يَلِدْ، وَلَمْ يُولَدْ، وَلَمْ يَكُنْ لَهُ كُفُوًا أَحَدٌ».

ثُمَّ لِيَتْفُلْ عَنْ يَسَارِهِ ثَلَاثًا، وَلْيَسْتَعِذْ مِنَ الشَّيْطَانِ، وَلْيَنْتَهِ، فَإِنَّ ذَلِكَ يَذْهَبُ عَنْهُ» (هذِه خُلَاصَةُ الأَحَادِيثِ الصَّحِيْحَةِ الْوَارِدَةِ فِي الْبُخَارِيِّ وَمُسْلِمٍ وَأَحْمَدَ وَأَبِي دَاؤُدَ)

"I believe in Allah and His Messenger. He is Allah, (the) One. *Allah-us-Samad* (السيد الذي يصمد إليه في الحاجات) (The Self-Sufficient Master, Whom all creatures need, He neither eats nor drinks). He begets not, nor was He begotten; And there is none co-equal or comparable unto Him." Then to spit over the left shoulder three times, seeking refuge from Satan, when this is done the temptation will pass. (Summary of *Ahadîth* collected by *Bukhâri, Muslim, Ahmad* and *Abû Dâwûd*)

One should say in response to this question that Allah is the Creator and that He has not been created, to make this easier to understand, we may say for example:

One comes before two, and nothing comes before one ... Allah is One, nothing comes before Him. As the Prophet ﷺ said:

«اَللّٰهُمَّ أَنْتَ الأَوَّلُ فَلَا شَيْءَ قَبْلَكَ» [رَوَاهُ مُسْلِمٌ]

"Allah, You are the First, there was nothing before You." (*Muslim*)

Q.18 What were the beliefs of the idolaters in Arabia before Islâm?

A. They use to pray to saints to earn their pleasure and intercession. Allah says (referring to their beliefs):

﴿ وَٱلَّذِينَ ٱتَّخَذُوا۟ مِن دُونِهِۦٓ أَوْلِيَآءَ مَا نَعْبُدُهُمْ إِلَّا لِيُقَرِّبُونَآ إِلَى ٱللَّهِ زُلْفَىٰٓ ﴾

"... And those who take *'Auliyâ'* (protectors and helpers) besides Him (say): "We worship them only that they may bring us near to Allah. ... (V.39:3)

﴿ وَيَعْبُدُونَ مِن دُونِ ٱللَّهِ مَا لَا يَضُرُّهُمْ وَلَا يَنفَعُهُمْ وَيَقُولُونَ هَٰٓؤُلَآءِ شُفَعَٰٓؤُنَا عِندَ ٱللَّهِ ﴾

"And they worship besides Allah things that hurt them not, nor profit them, and they say: 'These are our intercessors with Allah.' " (V.10:18)

Some Muslims also seek the intercession of saints thus imitating the idolaters.

Q.19 How do we eliminate (all traces of) *Shirk*?

A. *Shirk* cannot be completely eliminated unless we exclude the following:

1. The belief that others share in Allah's works such as the (*Sûfi*) belief that there are men called *Qutub* (قطب) who regulate the universe, even though Allah asked the idolaters:

$$﴿ وَمَن يُدَبِّرُ ٱلْأَمْرَ فَسَيَقُولُونَ ٱللَّهُ ﴾$$

"And who disposes the affairs?" They will say: Allah ..." (V.10:31)

2. The belief that others have the right to be worshipped, such as supplicating to the Prophets and saints for help etc. Allah says:

$$﴿ قُلْ إِنَّمَآ أَدْعُواْ رَبِّى وَلَآ أُشْرِكُ بِهِۦٓ أَحَدًا ﴾$$

"Say (O Muhammad صلى الله عليه وسلم): "I invoke only my Lord (Allah Alone), and I associate none as partners along with Him." (V.72:20)

Allah's Messenger صلى الله عليه وسلم said:

«الدُّعَاءُ هُوَ الْعِبَادَةُ» [رَوَاهُ التِّرْمِذِيُّ وَقَالَ حَسَنٌ صَحِيحٌ]

"Supplication is worship." (*Tirmidhi*)

34

3. The belief that others share in Allah's Attributes, such as the belief that the Prophets or saints have knowledge of the unseen, Allah says:

﴿ قُل لَّا يَعْلَمُ مَن فِى ٱلسَّمَٰوَٰتِ وَٱلْأَرْضِ ٱلْغَيْبَ إِلَّا ٱللَّهُ ﴾

"Say: None in the heavens and the earth knows the *Ghaib* (unseen) except Allah." (V.27:65)

4. Anthropomorphism (*Tashbîh*), comparing Allah's Attributes to humans, such as one who says: There must be a mediator between humans and Allah, to whom we address our prayers, just as one cannot meet the ruler or a higher authority (of a nation) except through a mediator, this is comparing the Creator to His creation, a form of *Shirk*. Allah says:

﴿ لَيْسَ كَمِثْلِهِۦ شَىْءٌ ﴾

"... There is none like unto Him ..." (V.42:11)

Allah says:

﴿ لَئِنْ أَشْرَكْتَ لَيَحْبَطَنَّ عَمَلُكَ وَلَتَكُونَنَّ مِنَ ٱلْخَٰسِرِينَ ﴾

"If you join others in worship with Allah, (then) surely (all) your deeds will be in vain, and you will certainly be among the losers." (V.39:65)

If one repents and eliminates these practices of *Shirk* and worship Allah Alone he will once again become a true believer in the Oneness of Allah . O Allah let us be among those who worship You Alone, do not make us to be idolaters.

Q.20 What are the dangers and punishment of *Shirk Akbar?*

A. *Shirk Akbar* condemns one to eternal damnation in Hell-fire, as Allah says:

﴿ إِنَّهُ مَن يُشْرِكْ بِاللَّهِ فَقَدْ حَرَّمَ اللَّهُ عَلَيْهِ الْجَنَّةَ وَمَأْوَىٰهُ النَّارُ وَمَا لِلظَّالِمِينَ مِنْ أَنصَارٍ ﴾

"... Verily, whosoever sets up partners in worship with Allah, then Allah has forbidden Paradise for him, and the Fire will be his abode. And for the *Zâlimûn* (polytheists and wrong-doers) there are no helpers." (V.5:72)

The Prophet صلى الله عليه وسلم said:

«مَنْ لَقِيَ اللهَ يُشْرِكُ بِهِ شَيْئًا دَخَلَ النَّارَ» [رَوَاهُ مُسْلِمٌ]

"And he who met Allah associating anything with Him entered (Hell) Fire." (*Muslim*)

Q.21 Are good deeds of any benefit to one who worships others besides Allah?

A. No, good deeds are of no benefit to those who worship others besides Allah. Allah says concerning the Prophets:

﴿ وَلَوْ أَشْرَكُوا لَحَبِطَ عَنْهُم مَّا كَانُوا يَعْمَلُونَ ﴾

"... But if they had joined in worship others with

36

Allah, all that they used to do would have been of no benefit to them." (V.6:88)

The Prophet ﷺ said: Allah says:

«أَنَا أَغْنَى الشُّرَكَاءِ عَنِ الشِّرْكِ، مَنْ عَمِلَ عَمَلاً أَشْرَكَ مَعِيَ فِيهِ غَيْرِي، تَرَكْتُهُ وَشِرْكَهُ»

[حَدِيثٌ قُدْسِيٌّ رَوَاهُ مُسْلِمٌ]

"I have no need of partners, whoever does any deed in which they associate partners with Me, I reject them and their partners as well."

VIII. MINOR *SHIRK* (*SHIRK ASGHAR*)

Q.1 What is *Shirk Asghar*?

A. Minor *Shirk* (*Shirk Asghar*) is to worship Allah so as to be seen by others. Allah says:

﴿فَمَن كَانَ يَرْجُواْ لِقَآءَ رَبِّهِۦ فَلْيَعْمَلْ عَمَلًا صَٰلِحًا وَلَا يُشْرِكْ بِعِبَادَةِ رَبِّهِۦٓ أَحَدًۢا﴾

"So whoever hopes for the meeting with his Lord, let him work righteousness and associate none as a partner in the worship of his Lord." (V.18:110)

The Prophet صلى الله عليه وسلم said:

«إِنَّ أَخْوَفَ مَا أَخَافُ عَلَيْكُمُ الشِّرْكُ الأَصْغَرُ: الرِّيَآءُ» [صَحِيحٌ رَوَاهُ أَحْمَدُ]

"What I fear most for you is *Shirk Asghar — Ar-Riya* (worshipping to be seen by others)." (*Ahmad*)

Included in *Shirk Asghar* is the saying:

"Were it not for so-and-so, it is Allah and so-and-so's will."

The Prophet صلى الله عليه وسلم said:

«لَا تَقُوْلُوا مَاشَآءَ اللهُ، وَشَآءَ فُلَانٌ، وَلَكِنْ قُوْلُوا: مَا شَآءَ اللهُ، ثُمَّ شَآءَ فُلَانٌ». [صَحِيحٌ رَوَاهُ أَحْمَدُ]

"Do not say: It is the Will of Allah and so-and-so,

38

rather say: 'It is the Will of Allah and then because of so-and-so'." (*Ahmad*)

Q.2 Is it permitted to swear by other's name besides Allah?

A. No, it is not permitted to swear by another name besides Allah. Allah says:

$$﴿ قُلْ بَلَىٰ وَرَبِّي لَتُبْعَثُنَّ ﴾$$

"... Say: Yes! By my Lord, you will certainly be resurrected... " (V.64:7)

The Prophet صلى الله عليه وسلم said:

$$« مَنْ حَلَفَ بِغَيْرِ اللهِ فَقَدْ أَشْرَكَ » [صَحِيْحٌ رَوَاهُ أَحْمَدُ]$$

"Whoever swears by anyone other than Allah, has associated partners with Allah (i.e. has commited *Shirk*)." (*Ahmad*)

The Prophet صلى الله عليه وسلم said:

$$« مَنْ كَانَ حَالِفًا، فَلْيَحْلِفْ بِاللهِ، أَوْ لِيَصْمُتْ » .$$
$$[مُتَّفَقٌ عَلَيْهِ]$$

"Whoever must take an oath should swear by Allah or keep silent (should not swear)." (*Bukhâri* and *Muslim*)

Swearing by the Prophets or saints is a major form of *Shirk*, if one believes that the saint has power to harm him. So we should refrain from taking such an oath, as this too is a major sin resulting in severe punishment.

39

Q.3 Should we wear good luck charms (like a thread or ring) believing that they have healing powers?

A. No, we should not wear them, since Allah says:

$$ ﴿ وَإِن يَمْسَسْكَ اللَّهُ بِضُرٍّ فَلَا كَاشِفَ لَهُ إِلَّا هُوَ ﴾ $$

"And if Allah touches you with harm, none can remove it but He,..." (V.6:17)

Hudhaifa saw a man wearing a thread around his hand to cure fever, so he cut the thread reciting Allah's Words:

$$ ﴿ وَمَا يُؤْمِنُ أَكْثَرُهُم بِاللَّهِ إِلَّا وَهُم مُّشْرِكُونَ ﴾ $$

"And most of them believe not in Allah except that they attribute partners (unto Him) i.e. they are *Mushrikûn* — polytheists." (V.12:106) (*Ibn Abû Hâtim*)

Q.4 Should we attach beads or shells etc. to our clothing to protect us from the evil eye?

A. No, we should not do that for protection from the evil eye, Allah says:

$$ ﴿ وَإِن يَمْسَسْكَ اللَّهُ بِضُرٍّ فَلَا كَاشِفَ لَهُ إِلَّا هُوَ ﴾ $$

"And if Allah touches you with harm, none can remove it but He, ..." (V.6:17)

The Prophet صلى الله عليه وسلم said:

$$ «مَنْ عَلَّقَ تَمِيمَةً فَقَدْ أَشْرَكَ» [صَحِيحٌ رَوَاهُ أَحْمَدُ] $$

"Whoever wears an amulet has committed *Shirk*." (*Ahmad*)
(An amulet — any object worn in the belief that it provides spiritual protection).

IX. INTERCESSION

Q.1 Through what may we seek intercession with Allah?

A. 1. The permitted and desired form of intercession is to supplicate to Him by His Names and Attributes, and by righteous deeds, and by seeking the blessings of the righteous (who are living), Allah says:

﴿ وَلِلَّهِ ٱلْأَسْمَآءُ ٱلْحُسْنَىٰ فَٱدْعُوهُ بِهَا ﴾

"And (all) the Most Beautiful Names belong to Allah, so call on Him by them... " (V.7:180).

Allah also says:

﴿ يَٰٓأَيُّهَا ٱلَّذِينَ ءَامَنُوا۟ ٱتَّقُوا۟ ٱللَّهَ وَٱبْتَغُوٓا۟ إِلَيْهِ ٱلْوَسِيلَةَ ﴾

"O you who believe! Do your duty to Allah and fear Him. Seek the means of approach to Him, ..." (V. 5: 35)

In his commentary on this verse Ibn Kathîr mentioned a *Hadîth* narrated by Qatadah: The Messenger صلى الله عليه وسلم said:

«أَسْأَلُكَ بِكُلِّ اسْمٍ هُوَ لَكَ سَمَّيْتَ بِهِ نَفْسَكَ»

[صَحِيحٌ رَوَاهُ أَحْمَدُ]

"I ask You by all Your Names, with which You call Yourself". (*Ahmad*)

And another *Hadîth* in which he ﷺ said to one of his companions who asked to be with him in Paradise:

«أَعِنِّي عَلَى نَفْسِكَ بِكَثْرَةِ السُّجُودِ» [رَوَاهُ مُسْلِمٌ]

"(You can) help me in this matter by frequent non-obligatory prayers." (*Muslim*)

Or follow the example of the three persons who were trapped in a cave (by a fallen rock) then they prayed to Allah mentioning their righteous deeds and Allah removed the rock and they were able to get out.

It is permitted to pray for intercession to Allah mentioning our love of Him or the love of the Messenger ﷺ and pious persons, since our love for them is also considered an act of good deed.

2. Forbidden forms of intercession: Praying to the dead, asking them for provisions and help, as is being done today. This is major form of *Shirk*, as Allah says:

﴿ وَلَا تَدْعُ مِن دُونِ ٱللَّهِ مَا لَا يَنفَعُكَ وَلَا يَضُرُّكَ فَإِن فَعَلْتَ فَإِنَّكَ إِذًا مِّنَ ٱلظَّالِمِينَ ﴾

"And invoke not besides Allah, any that neither profit you, nor hurt you, but if (in case) you did so, you shall certainly be one of the *Zâlimûn* (polytheists and wrong-doers)." (V.10:106)

3. As for praying by the Messenger's ﷺ name, such as saying: "O Lord by the Messenger ﷺ, heal me." This is an innovation which

was not practiced by the Prophet's صلى الله عليه وسلم companions. When ('Umar during his caliphate) sought the prayers of 'Abbas - the Prophet's uncle, as his closest living relative, he did not pray (for rain) seeking the intercession of the Prophet صلى الله عليه وسلم after his death.

Prayer such as this could lead to *Shirk* if it is believed that Allah needs a human mediator such as a human prince or ruler, since this is comparing the Creator to His creation.

Imam Abû Hanifa said:

وَقَالَ أَبُو حَنِيفَةَ: «أَكْرَهُ أَنْ أَسْأَلَ اللهَ بِغَيْرِ اللهِ».

"I dislike supplication to Allah through anyone but Allah. (*Ad-Durr Al-Mukhtâr*)

Q.2 Does any supplication to Allah require a human intermediary?

A.   No, a prayer does not require a human intermediary, as Allah says:

﴿ وَإِذَا سَأَلَكَ عِبَادِى عَنِّى فَإِنِّى قَرِيبٌ ﴾

"And when My slaves ask you (O Muhammad صلى الله عليه وسلم) concerning Me, then (answer them), I am indeed near (to them by My Knowledge)..." (V.2:186)

And the *Hadîth* of the Prophet صلى الله عليه وسلم :

«إِنَّكُمْ تَدْعُوْنَ سَمِيْعًا قَرِيْبًا وَهُوَ مَعَكُمْ»

[أَيْ بِعِلْمِهِ]   [رَوَاهُ مُسْلِمٌ]

43

"You pray to the One who hears all and is near, and He is with you (by His Knowledge)." (*Muslim*)

Q.3 **Is it permitted to ask for the prayer of those who are living?**

A. Yes, it is permitted to ask for the prayer of those who are living, but not from those who are dead. Allah said to the Messenger (when he was alive):

$$ ﴿ وَٱسْتَغْفِرْ لِذَنۢبِكَ وَلِلْمُؤْمِنِينَ وَٱلْمُؤْمِنَٰتِ ﴾ $$

"... And ask forgiveness for your sins, and also for (the sins of) believing men and believing women... " (V.47:19)

A *Hadîth* related by *Tirmidhi* says: A blind man came to the Prophet صلى الله عليه وسلم and asked: "Pray to Allah to heal me".

Q.4 **What is the mediation of the Messenger صلى الله عليه وسلم ?**

A. The mediation of the Messenger صلى الله عليه وسلم is the transmission of Allah's Message. Allah says:

$$ ﴿ يَٰٓأَيُّهَا ٱلرَّسُولُ بَلِّغْ مَآ أُنزِلَ إِلَيْكَ مِن رَّبِّكَ ﴾ $$

"O Messenger (Muhammad صلى الله عليه وسلم)! Proclaim (the Message) which has been sent down to you from your Lord... " (V.5:67)

In response to the testimony of the companions [during the farewell *Hajj* (pilgrimage)]·

«نَشْهَدُ أَنَّكَ قَدْ بَلَّغْتَ» [رَوَاهُ مُسْلِمٌ]

"We bear witness that you have transmitted the Message of Allah"

The Prophet ﷺ said:

«اللّٰهُمَّ اشْهَدْ»

"Allah, bear witness." (*Muslim*)

Q.5 From whom may we seek the Messenger's ﷺ intercession?

A. We may seek the Messenger's ﷺ intercession from Allah alone, as Allah says:

﴿قُل لِّلَّهِ ٱلشَّفَٰعَةُ جَمِيعًا﴾

"Say: To Allah belongs all intercession ..." (V.39:44)

The Prophet ﷺ taught his companions to pray:

«اللّٰهُمَّ شَفِّعْهُ فِيَّ» [رَوَاهُ التِّرْمِذِيُّ وَقَالَ حَسَنٌ صَحِيحٌ]

"O Allah grant him (the Prophet ﷺ) intercession for me." (*Tirmidhi*)

The Prophet ﷺ also said:

«إِنِّي خَبَّأْتُ دَعْوَتِي شَفَاعَةً لِأُمَّتِي يَوْمَ الْقِيَامَةِ، فَهِيَ نَائِلَةٌ إِنْ شَاءَ اللهُ، مَنْ مَاتَ مِنْ أُمَّتِي لَا يُشْرِكُ بِاللهِ شَيْئًا» [رَوَاهُ مُسْلِمٌ]

"I have kept unitl the Resurrection Day, my prayer

45

for intercession and that will be granted by Allah's Grace, for those of my followers who died worshipping none but Allah." (*Muslim*)

Q.6 May we request the intercession of the living?

A. We may request the intercession of the living in our worldly affairs only, as Allah says:

$$ ﴿ مَّن يَشْفَعْ شَفَاعَةً حَسَنَةً يَكُن لَّهُ نَصِيبٌ مِّنْهَا وَمَن يَشْفَعْ شَفَاعَةً سَيِّئَةً يَكُن لَّهُ كِفْلٌ مِّنْهَا ﴾ $$

"Whosoever intercedes for a good cause will have the reward thereof, and whosoever intercedes for an evil cause will have a share in its burden..." (V.4:85)

The Prophet صلى الله عليه وسلم said:

$$ «اِشْفَعُوا تُؤْجَرُوا» [صَحِيحٌ رَوَاهُ أَبُودَاوُدَ] $$

"Intercede for others and you will be rewarded". (*Abû Dâwûd*)

Q.7 Should we be excessive in our praise for the Messenger صلى الله عليه وسلم ?

A. No, we should not be excessive in our praise for him, as Allah said to the Prophet صلى الله عليه وسلم :

$$ ﴿ قُلْ إِنَّمَا أَنَا بَشَرٌ مِّثْلُكُمْ يُوحَى إِلَيَّ أَنَّمَا إِلَٰهُكُمْ إِلَٰهٌ وَاحِدٌ ﴾ $$

"Say (O Muhammad صلى الله عليه وسلم): I am only a man like you. It has been inspired to me that your *Ilâh* (God) is One *Ilâh* (God — i.e. Allah) ... ." (V.18:110)

46

The Prophet صلى الله عليه وسلم said:

«لَا تُطْرُونِي كَمَا أَطْرَتِ النَّصَارَى عِيسَى ابْنَ مَرْيَمَ، فَإِنَّمَا أَنَا عَبْدٌ، فَقُولُوا عَبْدُ اللهِ وَرَسُولُهُ»

[رَوَاهُ الْبُخَارِيُّ]

"Do not exaggerate in praising me as the Christians did for the son of Mary, for I am only a servant. So say (he is) Allah's servant and Messenger". (*Bukhâri*)

(Exaggerated praise of a human being is called: "*Itrâ*")

Q.8 Who was the first human creation of Allah?

A. The first human created by Allah was Adam, and the first thing created was the pen. Allah says:

﴿ إِذْ قَالَ رَبُّكَ لِلْمَلَٰٓئِكَةِ إِنِّي خَٰلِقٌۢ بَشَرًا مِّن طِينٍ ﴾

"(Remember) when your Lord said to the angels: Truly, I am going to create man from clay". (V.38:71)

And as the Prophet صلى الله عليه وسلم said:

«كُلُّكُمْ بَنُو آدَمَ، وَآدَمُ خُلِقَ مِنْ تُرَابٍ»

"You are all the children of Adam, and Adam was created from dust." (*Al-Bazzâr*)

The Prophet صلى الله عليه وسلم also said:

«إِنَّ أَوَّلَ مَا خَلَقَ اللهُ الْقَلَمُ»

[رَوَاهُ أَبُو دَاوُدَ وَالتِّرْمِذِيُّ وَقَالَ حَسَنٌ صَحِيحٌ]

47

"The first thing created by Allah was the pen" (This is after the creation of water and the Throne) (*Abû Dâwûd, Tirmidhi*)

Regarding the *Hadîth*:

«أَوَّل مَا خَلَقَ اللهُ نُورُ نَبِيِّكَ يَا جَابِرُ»

"The first thing Allah created (O Jabir) was the light of your Prophet" is a forgery, which contradicts the Qur'ân, *Sunna*, reason and revelation. As-Suyuti said of it: This (*Hadîth*) has no supporting chain of narration. Al-Ghamari said of it: It is a forgery. Al-Albani says: It is rejected.

X. *JIHAD* (FIGHTING), *WALÁ'* (LOYALTY) AND *HUKM* (RULE)

Q.1 What is the status of *Jihâd* for Allah's sake in Islâm?

A. *Jihâd* (fighting and struggle in the Cause of Allah) with one's wealth, and speech; according to one's ability is obligatory in Islâm. Allah says:

$$\text{﴿ ٱنفِرُواْ خِفَافًا وَثِقَالًا وَجَٰهِدُواْ بِأَمْوَٰلِكُمْ وَأَنفُسِكُمْ فِى سَبِيلِ ٱللَّهِ ﴾}$$

"March forth, whether you are light (being healthy, young and wealthy) or heavy (being ill, old and poor), strive hard with your wealth and your lives in the Cause of Allah." (V.9:41)

The Prophet صلى الله عليه وسلم said:

$$\text{«جَاهِدُوا الْمُشْرِكِينَ بِأَمْوَالِكُمْ وَأَنْفُسِكُمْ وَأَلْسِنَتِكُمْ»}$$

$$\text{[صَحِيحٌ رَوَاهُ أَبُودَاوُدَ]}$$

"Fight against the idolaters with your wealth, lives and speech" (according to your ability). (*Abû Dawûd*)

Q.2 What is *Walâ'* (friendship, loyalty)?

A. *Walâ'* (friendship, loyalty) is love and help of the faithful believers. Allah says:

$$\text{﴿ وَٱلْمُؤْمِنُونَ وَٱلْمُؤْمِنَٰتُ بَعْضُهُمْ أَوْلِيَآءُ بَعْضٍ ﴾}$$

"The believers, men and women, are *'Auliyâ'* (helpers, supporters, friends, protectors) of one another, ..." (V.9:71)

The Prophet ﷺ said:

«الْمُؤْمِنُ لِلْمُؤْمِنِ كَالْبُنْيَانِ يَشُدُّ بَعْضُهُ بَعْضًا»

[رَوَاهُ مُسْلِمٌ]

"The faithful believers are as a brick structure, each supporting the other". (*Muslim*)

Q.3 Is seeking the friendship and help of the disbelievers permitted?

A. No, seeking the friendship and help of the disbelievers is not permitted. Allah says:

﴿ وَمَن يَتَوَلَّهُم مِّنكُمْ فَإِنَّهُۥ مِنْهُمْ ﴾

"... And if any amongst you takes them as *'Auliyâ'*, then surely he is one of them ..." (V.5:51)

The Prophet ﷺ said:

«إِنَّ آلَ بَنِي فُلَانٍ لَيْسُوا لِي بِأَوْلِيَاءَ» [مُتَّفَقٌ عَلَيْهِ]

"The people of such-and-such clan are not my supporters (*Auliyâ*)". (*Bukhâri* and *Muslim*)

Q.4 Who is a *Wali* (friend)?

A. A *Wali* is a true believer, who fears and loves Allah very much. Allah says:

﴿ أَلَا إِنَّ أَوْلِيَاءَ ٱللَّهِ لَا خَوْفٌ عَلَيْهِمْ وَلَا هُمْ يَحْزَنُونَ ٱلَّذِينَ ءَامَنُوا۟ وَكَانُوا۟ يَتَّقُونَ ﴾

"No doubt! Verily, the *'Auliyâ'* of Allah [i.e. those who believe in the Oneness of Allah and fear Allah much (abstain from all kinds of sins and evil deeds which he has forbidden), and love Allah much (perform all kinds of good deeds which He has ordained)], no fear shall come upon them nor shall they grieve, — Those who believed (in the Oneness of Allah — Islâmic Monotheism), and used to fear Allah much by abstaining from evil deeds and sins and by doing righteous deeds". (V.10:62,63)

The Prophet ﷺ said:

«إِنَّمَا وَلِيِّيَ اللهُ، وَصَالِحُ الْمُؤْمِنِينَ» [مُتَّفَقٌ عَلَيْهِ]

"My only *Wali* are Allah and the most pious among the true believers." (*Bukhâri* and *Muslim*)

Q.5 By what sources do the Muslims govern?

A. Muslims govern by the laws laid down in the Qur'ân and authentic *Ahâdîth* (traditions and actions of the Prophet). Allah says:

﴿ وَأَنِ احْكُم بَيْنَهُم بِمَآ أَنزَلَ اللَّهُ ﴾

"And so judge (you O Muhammad ﷺ) between them by what Allah has revealed ... " (V.5:49)

Allah's Messenger ﷺ said:

«أَمَّا بَعْدُ، أَلَا أَيُّهَا النَّاسُ: فَإِنَّمَا أَنَا بَشَرٌ يُوشِكُ أَنْ يَأْتِيَ رَسُولُ رَبِّي فَأُجِيْبَ، وَأَنَا تَارِكٌ فِيكُمْ ثَقَلَيْنِ:

51

أَوَّلُهُمَا كِتَابُ اللهِ، فِيهِ الْهُدَى وَالنُّورُ، فَخُذُوا كِتَابَ
اللهِ وَاسْتَمْسِكُوا بِهِ»

" ... O my people, I am but a human being (soon) my Lord's Messenger will come to get me and I must answer him and I leave with you two great things, first, Allah's Book, containing guidance and light, so take Allah's Book and hold fast to it."

He ﷺ urged them to act upon Allah's Book and said:

«وَأَهْلُ بَيْتِي»   [رَوَاهُ مُسْلِمٌ]

"The second is my family." (*Muslim*)

The Prophet ﷺ said:

«تَرَكْتُ فِيكُمْ أَمْرَيْنِ لَنْ تَضِلُّوا مَا تَمَسَّكْتُمْ بِهِمَا:
كِتَابَ اللهِ، وَسُنَّةَ رَسُولِهِ»

[رَوَاهُ مَالِكٌ، وَصَحَّحَهُ الْأَلْبَانِيُّ وَمُحَقِّقُ جَامِعِ الْأُصُولِ
لِشَوَاهِدِهِ]

"I am leaving two things with you, you will never go astray if you hold fast to them. And they are: Allah's Book and the *Sunna* (traditions, sayings and actions) of His Messenger." (*Mâlik*)

XI. LIVING ACCORDING TO THE QUR'AN AND HADÎTH.

Q.1 Why did Allah revealed the Qur'ân?

A.   Allah revealed the Qur'ân so that it should be applied to our day to day lives, as Allah says:

﴿ ٱتَّبِعُوا۟ مَآ أُنزِلَ إِلَيْكُم مِّن رَّبِّكُمْ ﴾

"[Say (O Muhammad صلى الله عليه وسلم) to these idolaters (pagan Arabs) of your folk:] Follow what has been sent down unto you from your Lord [The Qur'ân and the Prophet Muhammad's *Sunna*],... " (V. 7: 3)

The Prophet صلى الله عليه وسلم said:

« اقْرَؤُوا الْقُرْآنَ، وَاعْمَلُوا بِهِ وَلَا تَأْكُلُوا بِهِ . . »

[صَحِيحٌ رَوَاهُ أَحْمَدُ]

"Read the Qur'ân and apply it, do not make your living from it." (*Ahmad*)

Q.2 What is the status of applying authentic *Hadîth* in Islâm?

A.   Applying authentic *Ahâdîth* is obligatory, as Allah says:

﴿ وَمَآ ءَاتَىٰكُمُ ٱلرَّسُولُ فَخُذُوهُ وَمَا نَهَىٰكُمْ عَنْهُ فَٱنتَهُوا۟ ﴾

"And whatsoever the Messenger (Muhammad صلى الله عليه وسلم) gives you, take it, and whatsoever he forbids you, abstain (from it), ..." (V.59:7)

53

Allah's Messenger صلى الله عليه وسلم said:

«عَلَيْكُـمْ بِسُنَّتِي وَسُنَّةِ الْخُلَفَاءِ الـرَّاشِدِيْـنَ الْمَهْدِيِّيْنَ، تَمَسَّكُوا بِهَا» [صَحِيْحٌ رَوَاهُ أَحْمَدُ]

"Hold fast to my *Sunna* and the *Sunna* of my rightly guided successors." (*Ahmad*)

Q.3 Is the Qur'ân alone sufficient for us without the *Hadîth*?

A. No, the Qur'ân alone is not sufficient without the *Hadîth*. Allah said (to the Prophet صلى الله عليه وسلم):

﴿ وَأَنزَلْنَآ إِلَيْكَ ٱلذِّكْرَ لِتُبَيِّنَ لِلنَّاسِ مَا نُزِّلَ إِلَيْهِمْ وَلَعَلَّهُمْ يَتَفَكَّرُونَ ﴾

"... And We have also sent down unto you (O Muhammad صلى الله عليه وسلم) the reminder and the advice (the Qur'ân), that you may explain clearly to men what is sent down to them, and that they may give thought." (V. 16: 44)

The Prophet صلى الله عليه وسلم said:

«أَلَا وَإِنِّي أُوتِيتُ الْقُرْآنَ وَمِثْلَهُ مَعَهُ»

[صَحِيْحٌ رَوَاهُ أَبُو دَاؤدَ وَغَيْرُهُ]

"Indeed I have been given the Qur'ân and along with it that which is like it." (*Abû Dâwûd* and others)

Q.4 Should we give priority to other opinions over the Word of Allah and His Messenger?

A. No, we should not give other opinions priority over

the Word of Allah and His Messenger, as Allah says:

﴿ يَٰٓأَيُّهَا ٱلَّذِينَ ءَامَنُوا۟ لَا تُقَدِّمُوا۟ بَيْنَ يَدَىِ ٱللَّهِ وَرَسُولِهِۦ ﴾

"O you who believe! Do not be forward (i.e. hasten not to decide) in the presence of Allah and His Messenger صلى الله عليه وسلم , and fear Allah..." (V.49:1)

The Prophet صلى الله عليه وسلم said:

«لَا طَاعَةَ لِمَخْلُوقٍ فِي مَعْصِيَةِ الْخَالِقِ»

[صَحِيحٌ رَوَاهُ أَحْمَدُ]

"Do not obey the created if it means disobeying the Creator". (*Ahmad*)

Ibn 'Abbas said:

أُرَاهُـمْ سَيَهْلِكُـوْنَ، أَقُـوْلُ : قَـالَ النَّبِـيُّ ﷺ، وَيَقُوْلُوْنَ: قَالَ أَبُوبَكْرٍ وَعُمَرُ». [رَوَاهُ أَحْمَدُ وَصَحَّحَهُ أَحْمَدُ شَاكِرٌ]

"My opinion is you will be ruined, if I say to you, 'The Prophet صلى الله عليه وسلم said ...' and you reply:'but Abu Bakr or 'Umar said ...' " (*Ahmad*)

Q.5 What should we do if we differ in the religious matters?

A. We should refer to the Qur'ân and authentic *Sunna*. As Allah says:

﴿ فَإِن تَنَٰزَعْتُمْ فِى شَىْءٍ فَرُدُّوهُ إِلَى ٱللَّهِ وَٱلرَّسُولِ إِن كُنتُمْ تُؤْمِنُونَ

55

بِاللَّهِ وَالْيَوْمِ الْآخِرِ ذَلِكَ خَيْرٌ وَأَحْسَنُ تَأْوِيلًا ﴾

"... (And) if you differ in anything amongst yourselves, refer it to Allah and His Messenger صلى الله عليه وسلم , if you believe in Allah and in the Last Day. That is better and more suitable for final determination." (V.4:59)

The Prophet صلى الله عليه وسلم said:

«تَرَكْتُ فِيكُمْ أَمْرَيْنِ لَنْ تَضِلُّوا مَا تَمَسَّكْتُمْ بِهِمَا:

كِتَابَ اللهِ وَسُنَّةَ رَسُوْلِهِ» [رَوَاهُ مَالِكٌ وَصَحَّحَهُ الأَلْبَانِي]

"I am leaving two things with you, you will never go astray if you hold fast to them. And they are: Allah's Book and the *Sunna* (traditions, sayings and actions) of His Messenger." (*Mâlik*)

Q.6 How do we demonstrate our love for Allah and His Messenger?

A. We love Allah and His Messenger by obeying and following their commands, Allah says (to the Prophet صلى الله عليه وسلم :(

﴿ قُلْ إِن كُنتُمْ تُحِبُّونَ اللَّهَ فَاتَّبِعُونِي يُحْبِبْكُمُ اللَّهُ وَيَغْفِرْ لَكُمْ ذُنُوبَكُمْ وَاللَّهُ غَفُورٌ رَّحِيمٌ ﴾

"Say (O Muhammad صلى الله عليه وسلم to mankind): "If you (really) love Allah then follow me (i.e. accept Islâmic Monotheism, follow the Qur'ân and the *Sunna*), Allah will love you and forgive you your sins. And Allah is Oft-Forgiving, Most Merciful." (V.3:31)

The Prophet صلى الله عليه وسلم said:

«لاَ يُؤْمِنُ أَحَدُكُمْ حَتَّى أَكُونَ أَحَبَّ إِلَيْهِ مِنْ وَالِدِهِ وَوَلَدِهِ وَالنَّاسِ أَجْمَعِينَ» . [مُتَّفَقٌ عَلَيْهِ]

"None of you have perfect faith until you love me more than you father, son, and all mankind." (*Bukhâri* and *Muslim*)

Q.7 Should we give up deeds and rely only on fate?

A. No, we should not give up deeds, as Allah says:

﴿ فَأَمَّا مَنْ أَعْطَى وَاتَّقَى ۝ وَصَدَّقَ بِالْحُسْنَى ۝ فَسَنُيَسِّرُهُ لِلْيُسْرَى ﴾

"As for him who gives (in charity) and keeps his duty to Allah and fears Him, and believes in *Al-Husna*, We will make smooth for him the path of ease (goodness)". (V.92:5-7)

The Prophet صلى الله عليه وسلم said:

«اعْمَلُوا فَكُلٌّ مُيَسَّرٌ لِمَا خُلِقَ لَهُ» [رَوَاهُ الْبُخَارِيُّ وَمُسْلِمٌ]

"Work (do deeds), for everything is easy for which it is created." (*Bukhâri* and *Muslim*)

He also said:

«الْمُؤْمِنُ الْقَوِيُّ خَيْرٌ وَأَحَبُّ إِلَى اللهِ مِنَ الْمُؤْمِنِ الضَّعِيفِ، وَفِي كُلٍّ خَيْرٌ، احْرِصْ عَلَى مَا يَنْفَعُكَ وَاسْتَعِنْ بِاللهِ، وَلاَ تَعْجَزْ، فَإِنْ أَصَابَكَ شَيْءٌ فَلاَ

57

تَقُلْ: لَوْ أَنِّي فَعَلْتُ: ... كَانَ كَذَا وَكَذَا، وَلَكِنْ
قُلْ قَدَّرَ اللهُ وَمَا شَاءَ فَعَلَ، فَإِنَّ لَوْ تَفْتَحُ عَمَلَ
الشَّيْطَانِ» [رَوَاهُ الْبُخَارِيُّ وَمُسْلِمٌ]

"The strong believer is better and loved more by Allah than the weak believer, though both are good, work hard for that which is beneficial for you and seek Allah's help, and do not give up. If you are stricken by misfortune do not say: 'If only I had done differently... ', rather say; 'That is what Allah decreed, He does as He Wills'. 'If only' opens the door to Satan's work." (*Bukhâri* and *Muslim*)

We learn from this *Hadîth* that the believer whom Allah loves (most) is the one who has strong belief and works hard for that which is beneficial and seeks help from Allah and he will do what all he can with the help of worldly means. If thereafter he does not achieve the desired effect, he has no regrets, but is satisfied with that which Allah has decreed for him. He says:

﴿ وَعَسَىٰ أَن تَكْرَهُوا۟ شَيْـًٔا وَهُوَ خَيْرٌ لَّكُمْ وَعَسَىٰ أَن تُحِبُّوا۟ شَيْـًٔا وَهُوَ شَرٌّ لَّكُمْ ۗ وَٱللَّهُ يَعْلَمُ وَأَنتُمْ لَا تَعْلَمُونَ ﴾

"... though you dislike it, and it may be that you dislike a thing which is good for you and that you like a thing which is bad for you. Allah knows but you do not know." (V.22:216)

XII. *SUNNA* AND *BID'AH* (INNOVATIONS IN THE RELIGION (ISLAM)

Q.1 Are there good innovations in the religion (Islam)?

A.   No, there are no good innovations in matters of faith, the proof is Allah's Saying:

﴿ ٱلۡيَوۡمَ أَكۡمَلۡتُ لَكُمۡ دِينَكُمۡ وَأَتۡمَمۡتُ عَلَيۡكُمۡ نِعۡمَتِي وَرَضِيتُ لَكُمُ ٱلۡإِسۡلَٰمَ دِينًا ﴾

"... This day, I have perfected your religion for you, completed my favour upon you, and have chosen for you Islâm as you religion ... " (V.5:3)

The Prophet صلى الله عليه وسلم said:

«إِيَّاكُمْ وَمُحْدَثَاتِ الْأُمُورِ، فَإِنَّ كُلَّ مُحْدَثَةٍ بِدْعَةٌ، وكُلَّ بِدْعَةٍ ضَلَالَةٌ، وَكُلَّ ضَلَالَةٍ فِي النَّارِ» [صَحِيْحٌ رَوَاهُ النَّسَائِيُّ وَغَيْرُهُ]

"Beware of new things (in matters of faith) for every new thing (in faith) is innovation, every innovation is darkness (error), and darkness (error) leads to Hell-fire." (*An-Nasa'i*)

Q.2 What is innovation in the religion (Islam)?

A.   An innovation in matters of faith is anything not based on evidence from Islâmic Law (*Shari'ah*).

Allah said in rebuke of the innovations of the idolaters:

﴿ أَمْ لَهُمْ شُرَكَـٰٓؤُاْ شَرَعُواْ لَهُم مِّنَ ٱلدِّينِ مَا لَمْ يَأْذَنۢ بِهِ ٱللَّهُ ﴾

"Or have they partners with Allah (false gods), who have instituted for them a religion which Allah has not allowed..." (V.42:21)

The Prophet صلى الله عليه وسلم said:

«مَنْ أَحْدَثَ فِي أَمْرِنَا هَذَا مَا لَيْسَ مِنْهُ فَهُوَ رَدٌّ»

[مُتَّفَقٌ عَلَيْهِ]

"Whoever adds some new things to our matters (religion Islam) which was not part of it, it will be rejected" (that is, it will not be accepted by Allah). (*Bukhâri* and *Muslim*)

There are many different types of *Bid'ah* (innovations), among them are:

(i) (*Mukaffarah*): Innovations which are rejection of the faith of Islâm: Such as praying to the dead or those who are not present and seeking their help, such as invoking them by saying, "O so-and-so help me."

(ii) (*Mahrramah*): Forbidden innovations: Such as Asking Allah's favor through the intercession of deceased saints, praying at graveside or taking oaths there, and building tombs over them.

(iii) (*Makruhah*): Disapproved innovations: Such as praying *Zuhr* (the noon prayer) after praying

60

Jumu'ah, praying aloud for blessings upon the Prophet صلى الله عليه وسلم after the call to prayer etc.

Q.3 Is there such a thing as *Sunna Hasanah* in Islâm?

A. Yes, there is. *Sunna Hasanah* are good practices (such as giving charity) which are sanctioned by the sources of Islâm. Allah's Messenger صلى الله عليه وسلم said:

«مَنْ سَنَّ فِي الإِسْلَامِ سُنَّةً حَسَنَةً فَلَهُ أَجْرُهَا، وَأَجْرُ مَنْ عَمِلَ بِهَا مِنْ بَعْدِهِ، مِنْ غَيْرِ أَنْ يَنْقُصَ مِنْ أُجُورِهِمْ شَيْءٌ...» [رَوَاهُ مُسْلِمٌ]

"Whoever introduces a good practice into Islâm will have the reward for it, and the reward of those who follow his practice thereafter, yet they will lose nothing of their reward". (*Muslim*)

Q.4 When will Muslims be victorious?

A. Muslims will achieve victory when they apply the Qur'ân and *Sunna* again in their lives, spread the teachings of *Tauhîd*, avoid all the different forms of *Shirk*, and confront their enemies with everything at their disposal. Allah said:

﴿ يَـٰٓأَيُّهَا ٱلَّذِينَ ءَامَنُوٓاْ إِن تَنصُرُواْ ٱللَّهَ يَنصُرْكُمْ وَيُثَبِّتْ أَقْدَامَكُمْ ﴾

"O you who believe! If you help (in the cause of) Allah, He will help you, and make your foothold firm." (V.47:7)

Allah also says:

﴿ وَعَدَ ٱللَّهُ ٱلَّذِينَ ءَامَنُواْ مِنكُمْ وَعَمِلُواْ ٱلصَّـٰلِحَـٰتِ ﴾

لَيَسْتَخْلِفَنَّهُمْ فِي ٱلْأَرْضِ كَمَا ٱسْتَخْلَفَ ٱلَّذِينَ مِن قَبْلِهِمْ وَلَيُمَكِّنَنَّ لَهُمْ دِينَهُمُ ٱلَّذِي ٱرْتَضَىٰ لَهُمْ وَلَيُبَدِّلَنَّهُم مِّنۢ بَعْدِ خَوْفِهِمْ أَمْنًا يَعْبُدُونَنِي لَا يُشْرِكُونَ بِي شَيْئًا ﴾

"Allah has promised those among you who believe, and do righteous good deeds, that He will certainly grant them succession to (the present rulers) in the earth, as He granted it to those before them, and that He will grant them the authority to practise their religion, that which He has chosen for them (i.e. Islâm). And He will surely give them in exchange a safe security after their fear (provided) they (believers) worship Me and do not associate anything (in worship) with Me... " (V.24:55)

The Prophet صلى الله عليه وسلم said:

«أَلَا إِنَّ الْقُوَّةَ الرَّمْيُ»

[رَوَاهُ مُسْلِمٌ]

"Strength is archery".

XIII. THE PRAYER (INVOCATION) WHICH IS ANSWERED

1. Allah's Messenger صلى الله عليه وسلم said:

«مَا أَصَابَ عَبْداً هَمٌّ وَلاَ حُزْنٌ فَقَالَ: «اللَّهُمَّ إِنِّي
عَبْدُكَ، وَابْنُ عَبْدِكَ وَابْنُ أَمَتِكَ، نَاصِيَتِي بِيَدِكَ،
مَاضٍ فِيَّ حُكْمُكَ، عَدْلٌ فِيَّ قَضَاؤُكَ، أَسْأَلُكَ
بِكُلِّ اسْمٍ هُوَ لَكَ، سَمَّيْتَ بِهِ نَفْسَكَ، أَوْ اَنْزَلْتَهُ فِي
كِتَابِكَ، أَوْ عَلَّمْتَهُ أَحَدًا مِنْ خَلْقِكَ، أَوِ اسْتَأْثَرْتَ بِهِ
فِي عِلْمِ الْغَيْبِ عِنْدَكَ أَنْ تَجْعَلَ الْقُرْآنَ رَبِيعَ قَلْبِي،
وَنُورَ بَصَرِي، وَجَلاَءَ حُزْنِي، وَذَهَابَ هَمِّي وَغَمِّي،
إِلاَّ أَذْهَبَ اللهُ هَمَّهُ وَحُزْنَهُ، وَأَبْدَلَهُ مَكَانَهُ فَرَحاً»
[صَحِيحٌ رَوَاهُ أَحْمَدُ وَابْنُ حِبَّانَ]

If a worshipper is struck by grief or sorrow and says this prayer, Allah will drive away his grief and sorrow and give him happiness in its place:
"Allah I am your worshipper, the son of your worshipper, my strength is in your Hand, my progress is in Your Command, just is Your Judgement, I ask you by each of Your Names, by which You have called Yourself or revealed in Your

63

Book, or which You have taught to one of Your creatures, or which You have chosen to keep in Your Secret Knowledge to make the Qur'ân the joy of my heart, the light of my eyes which removes my grief and drives away my sorrow thus replacing it with happiness". (*Ahmad, Ibn Hibân*)

2. Prayer of Yunus (Jonah) in the belly of the whale:

﴿ لَّآ إِلَٰهَ إِلَّآ أَنتَ سُبْحَٰنَكَ إِنِّى كُنتُ مِنَ ٱلظَّٰلِمِينَ ﴾

"... *Lâ ilâha illa Anta* [none has the right to be worshipped but You (O, Allah), Glorified (and Exalted) be You [above all that (evil) they associate with You]. Truly, I have been of the wrong-doers." (V.21:87)

«لَمْ يَدَعُ بِهَا رَجُلٌ مُسْلِمٌ فِي شَيْءٍ إِلَّا اسْتَجَابَ اللهُ لَهُ» [صَحِيْحٌ رَوَاهُ أَحْمَدُ وَغَيْرُهُ]

If any Muslim supplicates with this prayer, Allah will answer it. (*Ahmad* and *others*)

3. If the Prophet ﷺ صلى الله عليه وسلم was sorrowful he used to pray:

«يَا حَيُّ يَا قَيُّوْمُ بِرَحْمَتِكَ أَسْتَغِيْثُ» [حَسَنٌ رَوَاهُ التِّرْمِذِيُّ]

"Everliving, Everlasting Allah, in Your Mercy, I seek help". (*Tirmidhi*)